Meat and G......

Quick and Easy Ground Meat Recipes

BY

MOLLY MILLS

Copyright © 2021 by Molly Mills

License Notes

No part of this book may be copied, replicated, distributed, sold or shared without the express and written consent of the Author.

The ideas expressed in the book are for entertainment purposes. The Reader assumes all risk when following any guidelines and the Author accepts no responsibility if damages occur due to actions taken by the Reader.

Table of Contents

Introduction 6

The Secret to Delicious Ground Meat Recipes 9

    Korean Ground Beef Rice Bowl 12

    Vietnamese Ground Pork Rice Bowl 14

    Teriyaki Ground Turkey Rice Bowl 16

    Ground Pork Salad 19

    Swedish Meatballs 22

    Beef and Beans Chili 25

    Cheesy Chicken Patties 28

    Mediterranean Ground Lamb Bowl 31

    Beef Sliders 34

    Pork Dumplings 36

    Turkey Stuffed Bell Peppers 39

    Ground Pork Vindaloo 42

    Cheesy Meatball Bake 45

Spiced Ground Lamb and Lentils 48

Moroccan Meatball Soup 51

Ground Pork Stir-Fry 54

Shepherd's Pie 57

Turkey and Pumpkin Chili 60

One-Pot Ground Beef and Pasta 63

Hamburger Fried Rice 66

Mini Meatloaf 69

Sesame Ground Chicken 71

Wonton Soup 74

Creamy Ground Beef and Pasta 77

Orange Ground Chicken 80

Ground Pork Noodle Bowl 83

Chicken Picadillo 85

Shanghai Spring Rolls 88

Ground Turkey and Potato Casserole 91

Ground Beef Carbonara 94

Conclusion 97

About the Author 98

Don't Miss Out! 99

Introduction

Ground meat is a powerful ingredient that could help home cooks reign supreme in the kitchen and enjoy the family's approval in the process. Some say it can be dry and boring but with a little boost from a handful of herbs and spices and other ingredients, you can make ground meat extremely delightful. Take a peek at our ground meat recipe list and see for yourself. Here's the listing:

- Korean Ground Beef Rice Bowl
- Vietnamese Ground Pork Rice Bowl
- Teriyaki Ground Turkey Rice Bowl
- Ground Pork Salad

- Swedish Meatballs
- Beef and Beans Chili
- Cheesy Chicken Patties
- Mediterranean Ground Lamb Bowl
- Beef Sliders
- Pork Dumplings
- Turkey Stuffed Bell Peppers
- Ground Pork Vindaloo
- Cheesy Meatball Bake
- Spiced Ground Lamb and Lentils
- Moroccan Meatball Soup
- Ground Pork Stir-Fry
- Shepherd's Pie
- Turkey and Pumpkin Chili
- One-Pot Ground Beef and Pasta
- Hamburger Fried Rice
- Mini Meatloaf
- Sesame Ground Chicken
- Wonton Soup
- Creamy Ground Beef and Pasta
- Orange Ground Chicken
- Ground Pork Noodle Bowl
- Chicken Picadillo
- Shanghai Spring Rolls
- Ground Turkey and Potato Casserole
- Ground Beef Carbonara

Ground meat is more than just for your hamburgers and meatballs. It can make really amusing dishes, from rice bowls to pasta and bakes and soups. There are a lot of delightful uses for ground meat that you need to discover because they are quick and easy to make and even easier to appreciate.

The Secret to Delicious Ground Meat Recipes

In any recipe, the freshness of the ingredients is equivalent to none. That's also the key ingredient to ground meat recipes. If you want a delicious dish made of ground meat, make sure the meat is of excellent quality. And with that, we meant you start on the meat itself before it is even minced or ground.

Freshness is all that matters

If you have a butcher friend who will ensure that you are getting fresh meat each time, you are lucky. Fresh meat is slaughtered the same day. It has no foul smell, still very pink, firm, and not sticky. Ground meat is freshest if you are lifting from a freshly slaughtered animal to feed into the meat grinder. That does not mean packaged ground meats are bad. They can still be good enough, as long as you check if it was ground the same day.

Ground meat spoils faster than solid cuts. That's why you have to be scrupulous when picking a pack from the market. It makes all the difference.

Different Grind Size for Every Recipe

Apart from freshness, which is almost an obvious factor one has to secure when using ground meat, there is also the difference in grind sizes. You would find that some recipes require a meat mince, others say ground meat. The difference on the two is the size of the meat. Minced meat generally has bigger chunks than ground meat. When you ask your butcher to grind some meat for you, you may ask for a "once ground", which is not too fine or "double ground" if you need something that's fine enough. The specification depends on how chunky you need your meat to be in your recipe or how fine the recipe calls for.

Lean or Fatty?

Another important thing to note when buying ground meat is the amount of fat that goes in each pound. Normally, ground meats are made of leaner cuts. But you may also request a higher percentage of fat if your recipe requires it. This is basically a matter of personal preference. While some recipes may specify that the meat should be 90% lean or higher, you may opt for a fattier kind. It may not be necessarily healthy but it's tasty. That's for sure.

Proper Handling is Also Important

There are also a couple of tips and tricks that will help you ensure you are getting the most of your meats.

First, remember not to work up your meat too much. Minimize handling as much as possible before the meat hits the pan. Overmixing can make it tougher or firmer and less juicy.

Second, do not add salt early. It should come at the end of cooking. Adding salt early could draw out the juices from the meat.

Third, be creative and adventurous when choosing your marinade or seasoning. Ground meat is versatile. It will absorb any flavor you attach to it. A little experiment will go a long way as it will add some real excitement to your meals.

Well then, let's start!

Korean Ground Beef Rice Bowl

A good part of the globe has been taken over by the Korean fever and this wonderful dish will help heat things up even more. This dish is flavorful and is very easy to make. It is perfect for your family's weeknight meals because you only need about 20 minutes to put it together. Try this at home and get ready to do this often because it will surely be a favorite once they taste it.

Serving Size: 4

Prep Time: 20 mins

Ingredients:

- 1 lb. lean ground beef
- 2 cups cooked white rice
- 1 tbsp green onions, sliced
- ½ tsp sesame seeds
- 3 cloves garlic, minced
- 2 tsp sesame oil
- ¼ cup soy sauce
- ¼ cup brown sugar
- ¼ tsp ground ginger
- ¼ tsp red pepper flakes, crushed
- ¼ tsp pepper

Instructions:

Brown beef in a nonstick pan over the medium fire together with some minced garlic, breaking apart the meat into crumbles with the back of the spoon.

Meanwhile, whisk together sesame oil, soy sauce, sugar, ground ginger, crushed red pepper flakes, and pepper.

Add mixture to browned beef and let it simmer for about 3 minutes, stirring frequently.

Divide rice into bowls, spoon over ground beef mixture, and garnish with sliced green onions and a pinch of sesame seeds.

Vietnamese Ground Pork Rice Bowl

Now, here is another Asian rice bowl. But this time, it's from Vietnam and it's made of pork. This is another super-fast meal that is infused with the flavors of the cuisine's street food scene. This is absolutely a fantastic meal that you will love to enjoy, with rice, of course.

Serving Size: 4

Prep Time: 20 mins

Ingredients:

- 1 lb. ground pork mince
- 2 cups cooked rice
- 1 pc green onion, sliced
- 2 tsp ginger, grated
- ½ pc onion, finely diced
- 2 cloves garlic, minced
- 1 pc bird's eye chili, seeded and chopped
- 1 ½ tbsp vegetable oil
- 2 tbsp fish sauce
- 5 tbsp brown sugar

Instructions:

Heat oil in a wok on medium-high fire and sauté ginger, onion, garlic, and chili until fragrant.

Stir in pork and cook for about 2 minutes, breaking apart with the back of the spoon.

Sprinkle sugar and some fish sauce and stir. Cook until the pork caramelizes, stirring occasionally.

To serve, divide rice into separate bowls, spoon over cooked pork, and garnish with sliced green onion.

Teriyaki Ground Turkey Rice Bowl

Turkey makes for one great choice of ground meat. It comes out very tasty, especially after being treated to this sweet and delicious teriyaki sauce. It is also very healthy and easy for anyone in the family to love.

Serving Size: 5

Prep Time: 35 mins

Ingredients:

- 1 lb. ground turkey
- 4 cups cooked rice
- 1 cup broccoli, finely chopped
- 2 pcs carrots, peeled and grated
- 2 pcs green onions, diced
- ½ cup onion, diced
- 2 ½ tbsp garlic, minced and divided
- ½ cup soy sauce
- 2 tbsp red wine vinegar
- 1 tbsp vegetable oil
- ¼ cup water
- 1 tbsp cornstarch, dissolved in
- 2 tbsp warm water
- 1 tsp ground ginger
- 2 tbsp brown sugar
- 2 tbsp granulated sugar

Instructions:

Stir together soy sauce, vinegar, water, ½ tablespoon of minced garlic, ground ginger, and brown and granulated sugars in a pan and heat on medium. Continue whisking until the sugars are dissolved.

Whisk in cornstarch and warm water mix and cook until smooth and thick. Set aside.

Meanwhile, heat oil in a skillet or a wok on medium-high and sauté onions until translucent.

Add the remaining garlic, plus turkey and continue to cook for a few minutes, stirring often.

Add broccoli and carrots and stir for 3 more minutes until the veggies are crisp-tender.

Pour in prepared teriyaki sauce and simmer for 5 minutes, stirring occasionally.

To assemble, divide rice into individual bowls, spoon over turkey mixture, and garnish with diced green onions. Serve.

Ground Pork Salad

Here is a favorite dish in Thai cuisine. It is often made with different ground meats but in this particular recipe, we are using pork. This Ground Pork Salad is often served as an appetizer that can easily be converted into a main meal. The ground pork mixture, flared up with the flavors of lime and chilies, is served with lettuce leaves for wrapping. You basically spoon over the mixture into a piece of lettuce before putting it into your mouth. What an adventure, really!

Serving Size: 6

Prep Time: 40 mins

Ingredients:

- 2 lb. ground pork
- 1 large head lettuce, separated
- ½ cup cilantro, chopped
- ½ cup basil, chopped
- ½ cup mint, chopped
- 2 pcs shallots, minced
- 2 cloves garlic, minced
- 1 pc jalapeño, seeded and minced
- 1 cup salted peanuts, chopped
- 1 pc lime, sliced into wedges
- ½ cup lime juice
- 2 tbsp fish sauce
- 1 tsp Sriracha
- 1 tbsp vegetable oil
- 1 tsp light brown sugar
- Salt and freshly ground pepper

Instructions:

In a large bowl, hand mix pork with shallots, garlic and jalapeño. Set aside.

In another bowl, whisk together lime juice, Sriracha, fish, sauce, and brown sugar. Set aside.

Heat oil in a skillet on high and stir in the pork mixture, breaking up with the back of the spoon, for 5 minutes.

Turn off heat, pour in lime juice mixture, and set aside for about 5 minutes.

Transfer pork to a serving bowl, toss in herbs, season with salt and pepper, and garnish with peanuts.

Serve together with lettuce leaves and lime wedges for squeezing.

Swedish Meatballs

Meatballs commonly come to mind when there is ground meat. But this meatballs recipe is far from being ordinary. For one, it is made with not just one kind of ground meat but two: beef and pork. For another, it is served with mashed potatoes as an exquisite dinner when you want to impress your family. It's flavorful and soft, plays a nice treat to the plate.

Serving Size: 6

Prep Time: 45 mins

Ingredients:

- ½ lb. lean ground beef
- ½ pound lean ground pork
- 1 lb. russet potatoes, peeled, chopped, and boiled
- ½ cup onion, finely diced
- 2 cloves garlic, minced
- 1 tbsp parsley, chopped
- 1 pc white bread slice, finely diced
- ½ cup milk
- 1 pc egg, beaten
- 8 tbsp unsalted butter, divided
- ¼ cup + 2 tbsp heavy cream, divided
- 1 ½ cups beef broth, warmed
- 2 tbsp all-purpose flour
- ¼ tsp ground allspice
- ¼ tsp ground nutmeg
- Salt and freshly cracked black pepper to taste

Instructions:

Preheat the oven to 375 degrees F.

In a mixing bowl, soak bread in milk. Set aside.

Meanwhile, melt 2 tablespoons of butter in a pan on medium high and sauté the onions and garlic until fragrant. Transfer to the bread and milk mixture, stir, and let it sit for about 5 minutes.

Stir in ground meats, together with nutmeg, allspice, egg, salt, and pepper. Hand mix until well blended.

Form the mixture into meatballs and arrange them in a lightly greased baking sheet. Bake at the preheated oven for about 10 minutes or until cooked through.

Meanwhile, make the mashed potatoes by mixing together pre-boiled Russet with 2 tablespoons of butter and ¼ cup of heavy cream. Season with salt and pepper and mash to your desired consistency. Set aside.

To make the gravy, melt the remaining 4 tablespoons of butter in a pan on medium fire and sprinkle flour. Cook for about a minute.

Gradually whisk in broth, continue to simmer on low until smooth and thick, turn off the heat, then, add the remaining 2 tablespoons of cream and stir.

To serve, toss meatballs into the prepared gravy.

Spread out mashed potatoes in a large serving platter, top with the meatballs, drizzled with more gravy, plus freshly chopped parsley on top.

Beef and Beans Chili

Now, here is a classic chili recipe that will help warm you up during chilly nights. It's a quick and easy one-pot dish that's easy to make in a big batch. That's why it's a favorite dish to serve at parties or game day gatherings together with your favorite cocktail drinks. There may be a hundred and one ways to make chili in this generation but it is still quite fun to go back to the basics once in a while and enjoy the flavors that made us fall in love with the dish in the first place.

Serving Size: 6

Prep Time: 45 mins

Ingredients:

- 1 ¼ lb. lean ground beef
- 1 (14oz) can kidney beans, rinsed and drained
- 1 pc red bell pepper, chopped
- 1 (28oz) can diced tomatoes
- 1 pc onion, chopped
- 1 tbsp cilantro, chopped
- 1 tbsp green onions, chopped
- ½ cup cheddar cheese, shredded
- 2 tbsp chili powder
- 1 ½ tsp ground cumin
- 1 tbsp tomato paste
- 1 tbsp vegetable oil
- ¼ cup sour cream

Instructions:

Heat oil on medium high and sauté the onion and bell pepper until soft.

Stir in ground beef together with cumin, chili powder, salt and pepper. Cook until nicely brown, continuously stirring and breaking apart the meat with the back of the spoon.

Add tomato paste and stir for another minute.

Pour in diced tomatoes and kidney beans. Let it boil, then, turn heat to low and cook in a simmer for 20 minutes with the lid on.

Divide chili into individual bowls, garnish with cilantro and green onions, dot with sour cream, and cover with shredded cheddar.

Cheesy Chicken Patties

If you want your burger patties nice and light, turn to this chicken recipe that's made more delightful with the addition of cheese and broccoli. Hiding some veggies underneath is a great trick for smart homemakers to make the family eat healthily. That makes this a fantastic family meal idea to serve any weeknight. It's fast and easy to make, healthy, and utterly delicious, served with a yoghurt-ranch dip. What more can you ask for?

Serving Size: 4

Prep Time: 40 mins

Ingredients:

- 1 lb. ground chicken
- 2 cups broccoli, blanched and finely chopped
- ¾ cup shallots, finely chopped
- 1 clove garlic, minced
- 2 cups mozzarella cheese, shredded
- 1 pc egg
- ¼ cup olive oil
- ¾ cup panko breadcrumbs
- Salt and ground black pepper to taste

For the Yoghurt Ranch Sauce:

- 2/3 cup plain yoghurt
- 1/8 tsp chives
- ½ clove garlic, minced
- 1/8 tsp dried parsley
- 1/8 tsp dried dill
- ¼ tsp onion powder
- 1 tbsp lemon juice
- 1 tsp extra virgin olive oil

Instructions:

Preheat the oven to 375 degrees F. Prepare a parchment paper lined baking tray.

In a bowl, mix together chicken, broccoli, shallots, garlic, breadcrumbs, cheese, egg, and some salt and pepper.

Form mixture into small patties and arrange onto the prepared baking tray.

Brush top generously with olive oil and bake for 15 minutes.

After 15 minutes, flip the patties to the other side, brush again with oil, then, continue baking for another 10 minutes.

Meanwhile, whisk together the ingredients for the dip until well blended.

Serve the patties with the prepared sauce. Enjoy.

Mediterranean Ground Lamb Bowl

Here is another rice bowl but this time, it is infused with the delicate Mediterranean flavors. What makes it different? For one, it uses ground lamb. For another, it is served with flavorful side dishes like turmeric rice, hummus, pita bread, and freshly chopped veggies. It's a delightful meal altogether.

Serving Size: 4

Prep Time: 35 mins

Ingredients:

- 1 lb. ground lamb
- 1 cup turmeric rice, warmed
- 1 cup hummus
- 2 pcs pita bread
- 1 pc cucumber, peeled and diced
- 1 pc tomato, diced
- 1 cup feta cheese
- ¼ cup onion, finely diced
- 4 garlic cloves, finely minced
- ¼ cup fresh mint, chopped
- ¼ cup flat leaf parsley, chopped
- 1 tbsp olive oil
- 1 tsp allspice
- 1 tsp paprika
- ¼ tsp ground ginger
- ½ tsp red pepper flakes
- Salt and ground black to taste

Instructions:

Heat oil in a skillet or wok on medium fire and sauté the onions and garlic for about 5 minutes.

Stir in meat and cook until browned or cooked through.

Sprinkle allspice, paprika, ground ginger, red pepper flakes, salt, and pepper. Stir for another minute.

Turn off the heat and toss in parsley and mint.

To assemble, divide turmeric rice into individual bowls, top with cooked ground lamb, some hummus, cucumbers, tomatoes, feta, and pita bread.

Serve and enjoy.

Beef Sliders

For parties and everyday snacks, these Beef Sliders would certainly best them all. It's pleasing even to the most discerning taste and certainly, both adults and kids will love it. Everything about it is delightful, from the soft buns to, of course, the perfectly cooked patties made of ground beef and all the other additions that make it whole.

Serving Size: 6

Prep Time: 25 mins

Ingredients:

- 1 ½ lb. ground beef
- 12 pcs Hawaiian sweet rolls, split
- 12 pcs romaine lettuce leaves
- 12 pcs dill
- 3 pcs Cheddar slices, quartered
- 2 tbsp ketchup
- 1 tbsp yellow mustard
- 2 tbsp mayonnaise
- 1 tbsp vegetable oil
- Kosher salt and ground black pepper to taste

Instructions:

Preheat the grill on medium high and lightly grease the grill grates with some oil.

Divide ground beef to form 12 patties that are ½ inch in thickness.

Place on the grill, sprinkle with salt and pepper and then cook for about 3 minutes per side, turning once.

Place a slice of cheese on top and cook for a minute more.

To assemble the sliders, spread ketchup, mustard, and mayonnaise on the bottom side of the bread, top with a lettuce leaf, a patty, and a piece of dill. Repeat with the remaining ingredients.

Pork Dumplings

Now, let's make another amazing Asian recipe made specifically with ground pork. Dumplings are a big thing in Asia, particularly in Chinese cuisine. But it's also a big thing elsewhere. A lot of street food carts from all over the world have learned to carry dumplings as a quick and easy fare that people love munching on.

Serving Size: 8

Prep Time: 30 mins

Ingredients:

- 1 lb. ground pork
- 40 pcs dumpling wrappers
- ⅓ cup fresh cilantro, chopped
- ½ cup scallions, thinly sliced
- 1 tbsp ginger, minced
- 3 cloves garlic, minced
- 2 tbsp peanut oil
- 3 tbsp soy sauce
- 1 tbsp sesame oil
- ½ cup water

For the Dipping Sauce:

- ¼ cup rice wine vinegar
- ¼ cup soy sauce
- 2 tsp Sriracha sauce
- 2 tbsp sweet chili sauce
- 1 tbsp ginger
- ½ tsp sesame seeds

Instructions:

Stir together the ingredients for the dipping sauce in a bowl and set aside.

Hand mix pork with cilantro, ginger, garlic, soy sauce, and sesame oil in a large bowl.

Take a piece of dumpling wrapper, spoon over filling, and wet your finger a bit and press on the edges to seal. Continue until all the wrappers and filling are used.

Heat oil in a pan over medium fire and brown the dumpling in batches. Once all the dumplings are browned, put them all back to the pan and add water. Let it bubble for about 5 minutes.

Serve with a garnish of freshly sliced scallions and with the prepared dipping sauce on the side.

Turkey Stuffed Bell Peppers

Stuffed bell peppers are made healthier in this recipe with the use of ground turkey instead of ground beef. Apart from the slight tweak on the use of meat, this is everything you loved about the dish and more. It's protein-packed and has an enormous play on flavors, featuring quinoa, jalapeños, tomatoes, beans, cheese, and more.

Serving Size: 6

Prep Time: 40 mins

Ingredients:

- 1 lb. ground turkey
- 4 pcs bell peppers, halved and seeded
- 1 cup quinoa, cooked
- 1 (14oz) can black beans, drained
- 1 (14oz) can fire roasted tomatoes
- 1 pc jalapeño, minced
- 1 ½ cups pepper jack cheese, grated and divided
- ½ pc avocado, seeded and finely chopped
- 1 tbsp cilantro, finely chopped
- 1 tbsp green onions, finely chopped
- 1 pc onion, minced
- 3 garlic cloves, minced
- 2 tbsp taco seasoning
- ½ tsp salt

Instructions:

Brown ground turkey in a nonstick pan over medium fire, breaking up with the back of the spoon. Sprinkle with salt and cook for about 5 minutes, stirring often.

Add garlic and onions and continue stirring until the onions are soft and translucent.

Turn off the fire and add cooked quinoa together with 1 cup grated cheese, beans, minced jalapeño and tomatoes.

Sprinkle taco seasoning and mix until well blended. Set aside.

Meanwhile, preheat the oven to 350 degrees F.

In a baking sheet lightly greased with some cooking spray, arrange the bell peppers, skin side down.

Spoon over ground turkey mixture, top with the remaining cheese, then, bake for about 20 minutes.

Garnish with freshly chopped avocadoes, cilantro, and green onions before serving.

Preheat oven to 350°F. Using a sharp knife to cut the peppers in half lengthwise and then use a spoon to discard seeds. Next, line peppers on a lightly greased baking sheet.

Using a large spoon, divide filling equally between each bell pepper. Top with remaining cheese and bake for 20 minutes or until pepper is tender.

While still hot, top peppers with cilantro, avocado and green onions. Serve immediately.

Ground Pork Vindaloo

Get your instant pot ready for this delicious dish that is spicy and tangy and utterly delicious. It is an Indian comfort food highlight ground pork and some potatoes. As an instant pot recipe, this one is quick and easy and is prepared in just 20 minutes. That makes it the perfect dish on a busy weeknight for the entire family.

Serving Size: 4

Prep Time: 20 mins

Ingredients:

- 1 lb. ground pork
- 8 pcs small gold potatoes
- ½ tsp black mustard seeds
- ½ tsp cumin seeds
- 1 pc serrano pepper, minced
- 1 pc onion, diced
- 2 tsp ginger, minced
- 1 tbsp garlic, minced
- 1 tsp coriander, finely chopped
- 1 tbsp cilantro, finely chopped
- 2 tsp paprika
- ¼ tsp cinnamon
- ¼ tsp cayenne pepper
- 2 tbsp vegetable oil
- 2 tbsp apple cider vinegar
- ½ cup water
- 1 tsp salt
- ¼ tsp black pepper

Instructions:

Set the instant pot to 'sauté' and heat oil for a minute.

Stir in mustard seeds and cumin and let them brown a little.

Add onions and pepper, stirring frequently for about 5 minutes.

Put the ground pork, plus ginger and garlic. Let it brown for a few minutes, stirring often.

Add coriander, paprika, cinnamon, cayenne, salt and pepper and stir to blend.

Scatter the potatoes, then, pour in vinegar and water.

Close the lid and cook on 'high pressure' for about 10 minutes.

Release the pressure completely, transfer to a serving platter, garnish with freshly chopped cilantro, and serve.

Cheesy Meatball Bake

Take your meatballs recipe a notch higher by putting them in a baking dish, covering the top with lots and lots of cheese, and popping them in the oven. The result is a hearty and delicious comfort dinner that everyone, both young kids and adults alike, will surely adore.

Serving Size: 4

Prep Time: 50 mins

Ingredients:

- 1 lb. ground beef
- 1 lb. hot Italian sausage, casing removed
- ½ cup parsley, chopped
- 4 garlic cloves, minced
- ½ cup Parmesan cheese, grated
- 2 cups mozzarella cheese, shredded
- 1 cup Italian breadcrumbs
- 1 (24oz) jar marinara sauce
- 2 pcs eggs
- 1 cup milk
- 1 tsp salt
- 4 tbsp olive oil
- ½ tsp ground black pepper

Instructions:

Preheat the oven to 425 degrees F.

Stir together beef, Italian sausage, Parmesan, parsley, breadcrumbs, eggs, milk, salt, and pepper in a large bowl until well blended.

Divide mixture into meatballs.

Heat oil in a nonstick pan over medium fire and brown meatballs on all sides for about 3 minutes per batch.

Spread some marinara sauce in a casserole dish until the bottom is covered.

Add the meatballs, pour in the remaining sauce, and cover with mozzarella.

Cover the casserole with a sheet of aluminum foil and bake for about 25 minutes.

Remove the foil and broil for about 3 minutes until the cheese is completely melted.

Serve and enjoy.

Spiced Ground Lamb and Lentils

Lamb and lentils make a perfect combination, especially for a weeknight dinner that's easy to prepare and easy enough to be loved by everyone, including the picky young eaters. For the best result, add more or less of the red pepper flakes, depending on the level of heat that your diners can tolerate. Serve this over rice or with pita bread and you will surely keep everyone pleased.

Serving Size: 4

Prep Time: 35 mins

Ingredients:

- 1 tbsp vegetable oil
- ½ lb. ground lamb
- 1 ½ cups French green lentils, cooked
- ½ pc English cucumber, chopped
- ¼ cup parsley, chopped
- ½ cup cilantro, chopped
- 2 cloves garlic, thinly sliced
- 1 pc lemon, sliced into wedges
- 1 tsp red pepper flakes, crushed
- ½ tsp cumin seeds
- ¾ cup Greek yogurt
- Kosher salt and freshly ground pepper to taste

Instructions:

Heat oil in a wok on medium fire.

Sprinkle lamb with some salt and pepper and mix.

Divide mixture into patties and brown in oil for about 5 minutes per side.

Break up the lamb with the back of the spoon and stir in garlic, cumin seeds, plus red pepper flakes. Cook for about 2 minutes, stirring often, then, transfer to a bowl using a slotted spoon.

In the same wok, sauté lentils with some salt and pepper and cook for about 5 minutes.

Return lamb into the wok together with cucumbers, parsley, and cilantro. Stir and cook for another 2 minutes or more.

To serve, spoon yogurt in individual serving plates, spoon over lamb mixture, and garnish with more parsley and cilantro on top and lemon wedges on the side.

Moroccan Meatball Soup

Taste the exotic flavors of Morocco in this lovely soup that is hearty and delicious. In less than an hour, you can prepare this amazing recipe that bursts with a lot of different flavors. It is another favorite pick for a busy weeknight dinner.

Serving Size: 4

Prep Time: 40 mins

Ingredients:

- 1 lb. lean ground beef
- ½ cup whole-wheat couscous
- 4 pcs carrots, cubed
- 4 cups baby spinach
- 1 cup scallions, roughly chopped
- 1 ½ cups fresh cilantro, divided
- 1 pc egg, lightly beaten
- 1 tbsp extra-virgin olive oil
- 4 cups chicken broth
- 2 cups water
- 2 tbsp harissa, divided
- 1 ½ tsp ground cumin, divided
- Kosher salt to taste

Instructions:

Add about 1 cup of cilantro together with roughly chopped scallions in a food processor. Pulse until you make coarse puree.

Place half of the mixture in a large bowl, reserved half for later, and add ground beef, lightly beaten egg, 1 tablespoon each of harissa and cumin, plus salt. Mix until well blended.

Form the meat mixture into meatballs and set aside.

Heat oil in a pot or Dutch oven on medium fire, and sauté carrots for about 5 minutes.

Add the reserved cilantro and scallions puree, plus the remaining harissa and cumin and stir for another minute.

Pour in chicken broth and water and boil for about 2 minutes.

Add meatballs and let it simmer for about 8 minutes.

Stir in couscous and spinach and continue to simmer for another 5 minutes.

Adjust seasoning, toss in the remaining cilantro leaves, and turn off the heat.

Serve warm and enjoy

Ground Pork Stir-Fry

Ground meats are perfect for stir fries. They cook fast and would easily adapt any mix of flavors you add in. For this particular recipe, we are using ground pork and add a couple of veggies and spices to level up the taste. It's a quick, super easy, and inexpensive dinner option that the entire fam could love.

Serving Size: 4

Prep Time: 30 mins

Ingredients:

- 1 lb. ground pork
- 1 cup brown rice, cooked
- 1 cup carrots, julienned
- 1 ½ cups mushrooms, sliced
- 2 cups bok choy, chopped
- 2 cups spinach, chopped
- 3 tbsp ginger, peeled and grated
- ½ pc onion, sliced
- 2 garlic cloves, minced
- 1 tbsp green onions, sliced
- 1 tsp sesame seeds
- 3 tbsp soy sauce, divided
- ½ tbsp rice wine vinegar
- ¼ tsp cayenne pepper

Instructions:

Brown pork in a wok on medium-high for a few minutes.

Stir in a tablespoon of soy sauce and mix, breaking up the meat with the back of the spoon.

Remove meat with a slotted spoon and set aside.

In the same pan with some grease from the meat, sauté the mushrooms, onions, ginger, and garlic until fragrant.

Sprinkle cayenne pepper, then, pour in the remaining soy sauce, plus vinegar and spinach.

Put back the meat and cook until heated through.

To serve, divide the rice into individual bowls, spoon over meat mixture, and garnish with green onions and sesame seeds.

Shepherd's Pie

A favorite dish, especially during Thanksgiving, this Shepherd's Pie recipe can be made even on normal days. Why, it is made of pantry staples and ground meat, which is very easy to work with. Make this meal-in-one and impress your loved ones.

Serving Size: 6

Prep Time: 1 hr. 45 mins

Ingredients:

- 1 lb. lean ground beef
- 1 ½ lb. Yukon gold potatoes
- 3 pcs carrots, diced
- 1 pc cauliflower, separated into florets
- 1 cup frozen peas
- ½ lb. white mushrooms, sliced
- 2 tsp fresh thyme leaves, chopped
- 2 pcs onions, chopped
- 2 tsp olive oil
- 2 tbsp butter
- 2/3 cup lowfat milk
- 1 cup beef broth
- 2 tbsp all-purpose flour
- 1 tsp salt
- Freshly ground black pepper to taste

Instructions:

Brown meat in a nonstick skillet on medium fire for about 5 minutes. Remove to a plate using a slotted spoon and set aside. Discard the remaining grease.

Add oil into the same skillet and sauté the onions and carrots for 8 minutes.

Turn up the heat on high and stir in mushrooms and thyme leaves and cook for about 8 minutes.

Pour in broth, plus salt and pepper, then, simmer for 8 minutes.

Put the meat back into the pan and simmer for another 2 minutes, plus peas.

Transfer the mixture to a baking dish.

Preheat the oven to 350 degrees F.

Meanwhile, place the potatoes and cauliflower in a steamer basket and let it cook for about 10 minutes until soft.

Mash the potatoes and cauliflower together with butter, milk, and some salt and pepper.

Spread mashed vegetables on top of the meat mixture and bake for 25 minutes.

Turkey and Pumpkin Chili

Chili is another recipe that is best made with ground meat. In this version, we used turkey to make it fast and healthy. This recipe is best made during fall, when pumpkin is in season. The tasty flavors in the recipe are somehow balanced with the addition of sweet pumpkin.

Serving Size: 6

Prep Time: 30 mins

Ingredients:

- 1 lb. lean ground turkey
- 1 pc green bell pepper, chopped
- 1 (14oz) can red kidney beans, drained
- 1 (14oz) can white cannellini beans, drained
- 1 (14oz) can diced tomatoes
- 1 cup Tex-Mex cheese blend
- 1 tbsp cilantro, chopped
- ½ pc onion, chopped
- 3 garlic cloves, minced
- 1 (14oz) can pumpkin puree
- 1 cup chicken broth
- 1 cup Greek yogurt
- 1 tbsp olive oil
- ¼ tsp dried oregano
- 1 tsp smoked paprika
- 1 tsp ground cumin
- ½ tsp cayenne pepper
- 2 tbsp chili powder
- Salt and freshly ground pepper to taste

Instructions:

Heat oil in a pot or Dutch oven on medium high and sauté the onions until soft.

Stir in garlic and meat and cook for the next 5 minutes or until the meat is browned, breaking up the meat with the back of the spoon.

Add the rest of the ingredients, except for Tex-Mex cheese blend, yogurt, and cilantro.

Let the mixture boil and then, reduce heat to low and simmer for about 15 minutes.

To serve, divide chili into individual bowls, top with Tex-Mex cheese blend and cilantro. Dot with yogurt.

One-Pot Ground Beef and Pasta

Ground beef is perfect for pasta dishes. It mixes well with a lot of different ingredients and would cook fast to make a one-pot dinner in a snap. Try this at home and you will be surprised how many times you will get requests for this over and over again. And you certainly would not mind as it prepares in a snap—less than an hour!

Serving Size: 6

Prep Time: 45 mins

Ingredients:

- 1 lb. lean ground beef sirloin
- 12oz pasta
- 2 pcs carrots, peeled and sliced into three pieces
- 6 tbsp fresh basil, sliced
- 2 pcs onions, peeled and quartered
- 4 cloves garlic, minced
- ¼ cup Parmigiano-Reggiano cheese, grated
- 4oz fresh mozzarella cheese, sliced
- 2 tbsp tomato paste
- 1 (26oz) carton strained tomatoes
- 1 tbsp red wine vinegar
- 3 ½ cups chicken stock
- 1 tbsp olive oil
- 1 tbsp dried Italian seasoning
- ½ tsp red pepper flakes, crushed
- ½ tsp salt, divided

Instructions:

Preheat the oven to 350 degrees F.

Combine carrots and onions in a food processor and pulse until they are finely chopped.

Heat oil in an oven proof heavy bottomed skillet on medium high and add the carrots and onions mix. Sauté for about 4 minutes or until soft.

Stir in garlic and cook for another minute.

Sprinkle Italian seasoning, red pepper flakes, and half of the salt.

Add ground meat and cook until browned, about 5 minutes.

Add pasta, vinegar, tomato paste, tomatoes, about 4 tablespoons of basil leaves, and the remaining salt.

Boil, then, turn heat to low and simmer for about 12 minutes, stirring often.

Sprinkle cheeses on top and transfer the skillet to the oven and bake for about 15 minutes.

Serve with the remaining basil leaves as garnish.

Hamburger Fried Rice

This is one creative way to use ground meat and make sure it will be well received. It is a full meal-in-one because it has carbs, protein, and veggies as well. The secret to this delicious fried rice recipe, more than the ground beef, is the amazing play of flavors using a special sauce mix. Let's start!

Serving Size: 6

Prep Time: 35 mins

Ingredients:

- 8oz ground beef
- 4 cups white jasmine rice, cooked
- 4 pcs eggs, cooked sunny side up style
- 1 cup frozen peas
- 1 scallion, chopped
- 1 pc onion, diced
- 1 garlic clove, minced
- 2 tbsp vegetable oil
- ¼ tsp sesame oil
- 1 tbsp oyster sauce
- 2 tbsp soy sauce
- 1 ½ tsp dark soy sauce
- 1 tbsp Shaoxing wine
- ¾ cup beef stock, warmed
- ¼ tsp black pepper

Instructions:

Stir together dark and regular soy sauce, oyster sauce, sesame oil, beef stock, and freshly ground black pepper. Set aside.

Heat oil in a wok over medium fire and brown beef for about 5 minutes, breaking up with the back of the spoon.

Stir in garlic and onions, plus wine. Let the wine evaporate.

Pour in prepared sauce and simmer for a few minutes, scraping the bits at the bottom of the pan.

Add rice and stir fry until well-mixed.

Add peas and scallions and stir until heated through.

Serve in individual bowls with a fried egg on top.

Mini Meatloaf

Meatloaf is a very common dish that cooks think of whenever they have ground beef in the pantry. While it is a delicious dish, it can be pretty elaborate. To make mini versions of a meatloaf is a way to make it more suitable for serving at weeknight dinners. So here it is… let's cook!

Serving Size: 4

Prep Time: 1 hr. 10 mins

Ingredients:

- 2 lb. lean ground beef
- 3 pcs bacon slices, cooked and crumbled
- 1 cup carrots, peeled and finely grated
- 6 pcs green onions, thinly sliced
- ½ cup aged cheddar, grated
- ½ cup mozzarella cheese, grated
- 2 cloves garlic, minced
- 5 tbsp milk
- ½ cup dry breadcrumbs
- ½ cup ketchup
- ½ tsp paprika
- ½ tsp salt
- ½ tsp pepper

Instructions:

Preheat the oven to 375 F.

In a bowl, mix together carrots, cheddar, mozzarella, green onions, breadcrumbs, milk, ketchup, salt and pepper until well blended.

Add beef and all the remaining ingredients and mix well.

Divide into 8 meat loaves and arrange in an aluminum foil lined baking sheet.

Place in the oven for about half an hour until the meat is cooked through.

Sesame Ground Chicken

Take the amazing flavors of Chinese cuisine into your home with this sesame-laden chicken bowl. This dish is very similar to Soy-Sesame Chicken but it was leveled up by a few notches because ground chicken is used instead of large chunks. The small difference means big, cutting cooking time considerably without taking away any of its delightfulness.

Serving Size: 6

Prep Time: 20 mins

Ingredients:

- 2 lb. ground chicken
- 8 pcs green onions, sliced
- 2 tbsp toasted sesame seeds
- 2 tbsp ginger, grated
- 6 garlic cloves, minced
- 2 tbsp chili garlic sauce
- ½ cup soy sauce
- ¼ cup toasted sesame oil
- 1 tbsp sunflower oil
- 1 ½ cups chicken broth, divided
- 2 tbsp cornstarch
- ¾ cup brown sugar
- 1 tsp kosher salt

Instructions:

Heat oil in a wok on medium high and place ground chicken, plus some salt.

Let it cook for a few minutes, breaking apart with the back of the spoon, until the meat is no longer pink.

Add ginger and garlic and cook for another minute.

Stir in chili garlic sauce and sugar and let it cook for 1 minute more.

In a small bowl, whisk together 1 and ¼ cups of chicken stock, soy sauce, and sesame oil until well blended.

Pour sauce into the wok and let it simmer for a few minutes.

In another small bowl, dissolve cornstarch in the remaining ¼ cup of chicken stock.

Turn heat into medium low and add the cornstarch mixture a tablespoon at a time, until the sauce is smooth and very thick.

Fold in green onions and toasted sesame seeds and serve over hot rice.

Wonton Soup

Craving for some comforting Wonton Soup? Get ready to get down in the kitchen and work to make your very own. This recipe is not as difficult as it seems at first sight. In fact, you only need 35 minutes to make it and become a master!

Serving Size: 10

Prep Time: 35 mins

Ingredients:

- 1 lb. lean ground pork
- 1 lb. prawns, peeled and roughly chopped
- 50 pcs wonton wrappers
- 12oz dried egg noodles, cooked according to package directions
- 1 bunch bok choy, quartered and blanched
- 2 tbsp ginger, finely grated and divided
- 2 pcs shallots, finely chopped
- 2 cloves garlic, smashed
- 3 ½ tbsp Chinese cooking wine
- 3 tbsp toasted sesame oil
- 2 ½ tbsp light soy sauce
- 3 cups chicken broth
- 2 tsp sugar
- ½ tsp salt

Instructions:

In a large bowl, mix together pork and prawns, and salt plus 2 tablespoons each of shallots, Chinese cooking wine, and toasted sesame oil and 1 tablespoon of ginger.

Using a potato masher, gently mash the mixture until almost paste-like.

To wrap the wontons, lay a piece of wrapper in a flat work surface, spoon over filling and fold, sealing the edges securely.

Bring a large pot of water to a boil over medium fire and cook the wontons. Let it stay in rolling boil for about 5 minutes.

Remove the wontons using a slotted spoon.

Meanwhile, make the broth by stirring together chicken broth, garlic, sugar, and the remaining ginger, soy sauce, and wine. Let it simmer for a few minutes, add some of the liquid from boiling the wontons and adjust seasoning as needed.

To assemble, divide the wontons, noodles, and bok choy into serving bowls, ladle soup, garnish with the remaining scallions and toasted sesame oil, and serve immediately.

Creamy Ground Beef and Pasta

Here is another pasta and ground beef combo. But this time, we are leaning on the creamy side, which means it is rich and comforting. It is a classic recipe that is undeniably pleasing and definitely loveable. Serve this with some garlic bread and you will surely impress everyone at the dining table.

Serving Size: 8

Prep Time: 30 mins

Ingredients:

- 2 lb. lean ground beef
- 1 lb. Rotini pasta, cooked according to package instructions
- 2 cups sharp cheddar cheese, grated
- 1 tbsp parsley, finely chopped
- 1 pc yellow onion, diced
- 3 garlic cloves, minced
- 1 (28oz) can tomato sauce
- 1 cup heavy cream
- 1 cup beef broth
- 2 tbsp olive oil
- ¼ cup flour
- 1 tsp dried oregano
- 1 tsp dried basil
- ½ tsp red pepper flakes, crushed
- 2 tsp kosher salt

Instructions:

Heat onion in a pan on medium fire and sauté the onions until soft and translucent.

Stir in beef and cook until browned, breaking apart with the back of the spoon.

Remove with a slotted spoon, discard much of the grease, then, put back the meat together with garlic, oregano, basil, red pepper flakes, and salt.

Sprinkle flour and cook for another minute, stirring constantly.

Pour tomato sauce and broth and let it simmer for about 15 minutes.

Stir in cream and pasta and simmer for a few more minutes.

Toss in cheese and let it melt a little.

Serve with a garnish of freshly chopped parsley.

Orange Ground Chicken

Remember Orange Chicken? This is the version where we are using ground chicken instead to make the process faster. It's a very simple recipe that is both sweet and savory. Perfected with delicate Asian flavors. This is another way to play around with ground meat and create an interesting dish that everyone in the family would truly enjoy.

Serving Size: 6

Prep Time: 30 mins

Ingredients:

- 1 ½ lb. ground chicken
- 3 cups cooked rice
- 1 tbsp green onions, chopped
- 4 tsp fresh orange juice
- ½ cup soy sauce
- 4 tsp rice wine vinegar
- 2 tsp cider vinegar
- ¼ tsp sesame oil
- 1 tsp orange zest
- 3 tsp ground ginger
- 4 tsp garlic, minced
- ½ tsp dried chili peppers
- ¼ cup cold water
- 5 tbsp cornstarch
- 2/3 cup white sugar

Instructions:

Stir together orange juice, soy sauce, cider and rice wine vinegars, sesame oil, orange zest, ginger, garlic, dried chili pepper, and sugar in a bowl. Set aside.

Meanwhile, heat oil in a pan over medium fire and brown ground chicken, stirring often.

Add prepared sauce and let it boil, then, turn heat to low and simmer for a few minutes.

Dissolve cornstarch in water and add it into the pan. Stir until the sauce is smooth and thick.

To serve, divide rice evenly among serving bowls, spoon over chicken mixture, and garnish with sliced green onions.

Ground Pork Noodle Bowl

Here is something you could do to rock the dining table. It's a mix of ground pork and noodles in a delicious miso-laden soup. It has Asian influences and you will surely be delighted at the comforting warmth it will provide your tummy. It's another fantastic weeknight dinner idea, especially when the weather is chilly.

Serving Size: 4

Prep Time: 20 mins

Ingredients:

- 8oz ground pork
- 8oz brown rice noodles, cooked according to package directions
- 1 cup carrots, sliced into matchsticks
- ½ cup scallions, sliced
- 8oz mushrooms, sliced
- 3 tbsp yellow onion, peeled and grated
- 2 tbsp white miso
- 1 tbsp chili garlic sauce
- 2 cups beef stock
- 1 tbsp soy sauce

Instructions:

Brown pork in a nonstick pan over medium-high fire until no longer pink.

Add mushrooms and onions and stir for 10 minutes.

Toss in carrots, miso, chili garlic sauce, soy sauce, and beef stock. Let it boil for 3 minutes, or until the carrots are crisp tender.

To serve, divide cooked noodles among individual bowls, ladle ground pork mixture, and garnish with freshly sliced scallions.

Chicken Picadillo

Picadillo is a Cuban dish made primarily with ground pork plus a handful of herbs and aromatics. In this healthier version, we substitute pork with chicken but maintains the rest of the ingredients that make it a vibrant and flavorful dish. Bell peppers, oregano, carrots, olives, and more—those are just some of the nice things you can find in the bowl.

Serving Size: 8

Prep Time: 30 mins

Ingredients:

- 2 lb. ground chicken
- 1 cup carrots, sliced into matchsticks
- 2 pcs bell peppers, seeded and diced
- 1 pc onion, chopped
- ½ cup Spanish olives with pimento, sliced
- ¾ cup currants
- 2 pcs bay leaves
- 1 tsp garlic, minced
- 1 (14.5oz) can diced tomatoes
- 8oz tomato sauce
- 1 tbsp olive oil
- 1 cup dry white wine
- 2 tbsp balsamic vinegar
- 2 tsp ground cumin
- 1 ½ tsp sea salt
- Pinch of freshly ground black pepper

Instructions:

Heat oil in a pot or Dutch oven on medium high and brown meat, breaking apart with the back of the spoon and stirring frequently until it is no longer pink.

Stir in onions and garlic and cook for about 5 minutes.

Add carrots and bell peppers and let it cook for another 3 minutes or until the vegetables are crisp tender.

Add the rest of the ingredients and let it boil, then, turn heat to low and continue cooking in a simmer for about 15 minutes.

Remove bay leaves, adjust seasoning as needed, and serve warm over rice.

Shanghai Spring Rolls

Inspired by the colorful and vibrant Shanghai cuisine, this dish is a great food for all occasions. You can serve it for your family dinners or make it part of your buffet spread. A lot of people appreciate the flavorful ground pork filling paired with a crispy fried wrapper. It's nicely balanced and very delicious.

Serving Size: 24

Prep Time: 1 hr. 45 mins

Ingredients:

- 2/3 cup lean ground pork
- 24 pcs spring roll wrappers
- 1 pc napa cabbage, shredded
- 8 pcs dried shiitake mushrooms, soaked and sliced
- 2 ½ tbsp Shaoxing wine, divided
- ½ tsp soy sauce
- 2 ½ tsp sesame oil, divided
- 2 ¼ cups vegetable oil, divided
- 1 ½ tbsp cornstarch, dissolved in
- 1 tbsp water
- ½ tsp cornstarch
- Salt and ground white pepper to taste

Instructions:

Hand mix pork, ½ tablespoon of wine, ½ teaspoon sesame oil, cornstarch, salt, and white pepper in a bowl. Cover with a sheet of plastic wrap and set aside.

Heat about ¼ cup of oil in a pan and add pork with the marinade. Cook until browned, stirring frequently.

Stir in mushrooms and cabbage and cook for another few minutes.

Add the remaining wine and sesame oil, plus soy sauce. Adjust seasoning as needed. Pour in cornstarch and water mixture and let it bubble until thickened.

Transfer to a bowl and set aside to cool completely.

Once cooled, place a spring roll wrapper in a flat surface, spoon over filling and wrap tightly, keeping both ends secure, similar to a cigar shape. Repeat with the remaining wrappers and filling.

Heat the remaining oil in a pan on medium fire and fry spring rolls until nicely brown and crispy.

Drain excess oil on paper towels and serve with your favorite dipping sauce.

Ground Turkey and Potato Casserole

This turkey and potato casserole is another quick and easy dinner recipe that you can make for your family. It's healthy and satisfying and very delicious. It is almost like a Picadillo but it's mostly made of pantry staples, so you can find it easy to make whenever you feel like doing it.

Serving Size: 4

Prep Time: 25 mins

Ingredients:

- 1 lb. ground turkey
- 4 cups potatoes, diced
- 2 tsp garlic, minced
- 1 (8oz) can tomato sauce
- 2 tbsp olive oil
- ½ cup water
- ½ tsp dried parsley
- ½ tsp chili powder
- 1 tsp dried basil
- 1 ½ tsp dried oregano, divided
- ½ tsp onion powder
- ½ tsp garlic powder
- Salt and freshly ground black pepper to taste

Instructions:

Brown meat in a nonstick skillet over medium fire, breaking apart the meat with the back of the spoon and stirring occasionally.

Season with ½ teaspoon of oregano, garlic and chili powder, plus salt and pepper.

Remove with a slotted spoon and set aside.

Meanwhile, add oil into the same skillet and sauté potatoes on medium fire, stirring frequently.

Put back turkey and add the rest of the ingredients.

Let it boil, then, turn heat to low and continue cooking in a simmer until the potatoes are tender.

Serve and enjoy.

Ground Beef Carbonara

Carbonara is a classic dish that is so easy to love. A lot of people like it because it is pretty simple but satisfying. In this recipe, we are taking carbonara to a different level with the addition of round meat. This one prepares in about half an hour, so you will have more time to enjoy the meal with the family.

Serving Size: 6

Prep Time: 30 mins

Ingredients:

- ½ lb. lean ground beef
- 12oz spaghetti, cooked according to package directions
- 4 pcs bacon slices
- 3 cups mushrooms, sliced
- 1 pc onion, chopped
- 4 garlic cloves, finely chopped
- 1 cup Parmesan cheese, grated
- 2 tbsp parsley, chopped
- 1 cup whipping cream
- 3 pcs pasteurized eggs, beaten
- ½ tsp salt
- ¼ tsp ground black pepper

Instructions:

Cook bacon in a nonstick skillet until lightly brown and crispy.

Transfer to a paper-towel lined plate to drain excess grease, then, crumble.

In the same skillet with some of the bacon grease, brown beef for about 5 minutes.

Add mushrooms and onions and stir for another 5 minutes.

Stir in garlic and season with salt and pepper.

Toss in pasta and cream, plus bacon and eggs, turn heat to low, and stir to blend.

Add cheese and let it become melty.

Garnish top with freshly chopped parsley and serve.

Conclusion

Ground meat is pretty easy to handle and turns into a handful of delicious recipes. They are also interchangeable. You can choose any type of ground meat that you like and use it according to your preference and its availability. This cookbook has 30 different recipes and even if it calls for a particular type of ground meat, you can easily substitute it with whatever you like or whatever is on hand. They may not exactly taste the same but the difference would not matter that much.

Ground meats, although different in fibers and in cooking requirements, normally taste almost the same. With its size, it often adapts the flavor of the rest of the ingredients easily. So whether you make a meatloaf with ground pork or beef or chicken and others, the flavor will remain. If there are any differences, it would just be the cooking time and how healthy your dish is. Ground chicken and turkey are considered healthier compared to red meats.

We hope you enjoy this trip through 30 ground meat recipes that are quick and easy to make and much easier to love as well, whether you are feeding it to a toddler or an adult. Even picky eaters could learn to adore these ground meat recipes. They are not only bursting with delicious flavors but are also easy to chew and satisfy, even the most discerning tastes.

Happy cooking!

About the Author

Molly Mills always knew she wanted to feed people delicious food for a living. Being the oldest child with three younger brothers, Molly learned to prepare meals at an early age to help out her busy parents. She just seemed to know what spice went with which meat and how to make sauces that would dress up the blandest of pastas. Her creativity in the kitchen was a blessing to a family where money was tight and making new meals every day was a challenge.

Molly was also a gifted athlete as well as chef and secured a Lacrosse scholarship to Syracuse University. This was a blessing to her family as she was the first to go to college and at little cost to her parents. She took full advantage of her college education and earned a business degree. When she graduated, she joined her culinary skills and business acumen into a successful catering business. She wrote her first e-book after a customer asked if she could pay for several of her recipes. This sparked the entrepreneurial spirit in Mills and she thought if one person wanted them, then why not share the recipes with the world!

Molly lives near her family's home with her husband and three children and still cooks for her family every chance she gets. She plays Lacrosse with a local team made up of her old teammates from college and there are always some tasty nibbles on the ready after each game.

Don't Miss Out!

Scan the QR-Code below and you can sign up to receive emails whenever Molly Mills publishes a new book. There's no charge and no obligation.

Sign Me Up

https://molly.gr8.com

Made in United States
Troutdale, OR
01/12/2024

16921416R00058